DISCOVERING WHO GOD CREATED ME TO BE AND MY PURPOSE IN LIFE

KIMBERLY ROSS GLASPER

DEDICATION

"The Lord is my light and my salvation whom shall I fear?"
— Psalm 27:1

I dedicate this book to my Lord and Savior, Jesus Christ, who became my Light in every dark place and my Strength in every weak moment.

To my children, Alexis and Tyree, you are the living reminders of God's promises fulfilled.

May everyone who reads these pages discover what I discovered that His light never fails, His grace never runs out, and His love never let's go.

TABLE OF CONTENTS

ABOUT THE AUTHOR

I was born in the small town of Hayti, Missouri, where my early life was shaped by family, faith, and the quiet strength that comes from small-town living. Now, at 56 years old, I am the proud mother of two wonderful adult children, Alexus and Tyree, who remain my greatest blessings and the foundation of my resilience.

My journey has been one of faith, perseverance, and transformation. From navigating life's valleys to discovering my God-given purpose, I have learned firsthand what it truly means to trust Christ through every season. I am a woman who has survived emotional battles, embraced spiritual awakening, and risen into my calling with courage and conviction.

Today, I use my voice and testimony to inspire others to seek healing, build their faith, and walk confidently in the love of Christ. My life is proof that no matter where you begin, God can breathe purpose into your pain and turn every struggle into a stepping stone toward destiny. With a heart for service and a passion for encouraging others, I strive to shine as a light for those searching for hope, peace, and spiritual direction..

INTRODUCTION

A LIFE OF FAITH, STRUGGLE & SURVIVAL

I am Kimberly Ross & my life story does not only talk about battling the world's cruelties but also about praising a life rooted in faith, amid harsh trials & coming out of those unthinkable hardships being not perfectly whole, but transformed. My life story is a light of hope for people, lacking resilience & hope in God to crush challenges lined in their ways. My childhood experiences in Hayti, Missouri, to my current place in Justice, Illinois, exhibit a journey of huge challenges as well as victories.

My story gives you a roller-coaster ride through moments of disappointment and happiness, laced together. From fighting with mental health issues to exploring prayer's power, I have dealt with personal hardships that most can never even imagine. But through each sadness, I discerned strength that I attribute to God's grace, not myself. Through my experiences, I learned that while life might be anxious with difficulty, it paves a way for us to explore our purpose, strength to never get frayed from the bombardment of hardships in our lives.

In this book, you will find my awakening to my divine calling, right from the anxiety & depression to the greatest heights of spiritual clarification. Through my faith & determination, I skilled myself, not just to survive, but to thrive with confidence. Let me grab your hand to walk together through every twist, turn, trial, and victory of mine, and end up with discerning something productive in yourself to deal with your challenges & stand out in every walk of life.

CHAPTER 1

ROOTS IN MISSOURI & FAMILY LESSONS

My life began in the small town of Hayti, Missouri, in Pemiscot County. It is the town where everyone knows everyone else, the pace of life is slow & the challenge to rise above the normal is intense. But for me, the foundation of my faith was first laid. Influenced by a Christian-centric environment at home led by my parents, Ernest Glasper and Berta, I explored the path of spirituality.

My father, having great faith, used to pray every night, and that also left an influence on me. Though the praying act was very simple, it hinted at his belief in God. His nightly devotions made a foundation for me to understand faith in God. Amid this perfect spiritual devotion, my family's life was not calm. There were intense hardships illness, financial crises & family dynamics were affected with tension.

While parents were the breadwinners of a family, the disturbance in the house was huge. My siblings, each dealing with their own issues, created an often muddled & stressful environment in the house. But amid the turbulence, I found succor in my father's nightly prayers. In those calm moments, there was a great reminder that faith could ensure a refuge no matter how tough life was. Though the rest of my family dealt with different challenges, my father's prayers were also the protective shield against the invisible hardships that would have been unbearable if they had hit us along with the visible challenges of our time.

Despite the love & care of my parents, my childhood was influenced by a search for identity. I heard the scriptures & attended church services, but the whispering in my ears was noticeable, reminding me of something missing. I was caught in the cultural pull of peer pressure & youthful rebellion, hunting for meaning outside the walls of my childhood home. Like many teenagers, I was disconnected from the faith that had been introduced in me.

At that point in time, I faced one of my initial challenges with identity, feeling damaged between the faith that had been my greater foundation & the outside world that was to promise more fun & fulfillment. I visited the church because I had to, not because it was a spiritual awakening for me. However, the seeds my father had planted would not be uprooted simply. They lay dormant for years, waiting for the correct time to bloom.

Having studied in high school, I moved to Chicago, hunting for opportunities for education & work. But I carried the lessons of upbringing, particularly that God was always present, even when I didn't feel His presence. Furthermore, Chicago brought its own specific challenges, and keeping that in mind, I began the process of rediscovery of myself and my faith.

CHAPTER 2

A NEW BEGINNING IN CHICAGO

Leaving Missouri was one of the hardest choices I ever made, but deep down, I knew it was necessary. The city of Hayti served as my home and foundation until deep within I sensed that divine plans existed for my life. The bus to Chicago carried me forward as I left behind my possessions, but brought with me a heart full of dreams and a mix of nervousness and trust. The path ahead remains uncertain, but I must leave this place behind. God leads us to leave our comfortable places so we can discover the hidden power that exists within us.

When I arrived in Chicago, the city felt alive in a way Missouri never had. The streets were loud, filled with people rushing to places I couldn't yet imagine belonging to. The buildings reached high into the sky above me while everything around me seemed to speed up including the traffic, the conversations, and even the passage of time. I went from slow country mornings to sleepless city nights, and though I felt small, I also felt a stirring in my soul. It was as if God had placed me in the middle of something bigger than I could comprehend, a new chapter waiting to unfold.

My first few months were difficult. The rental expenses were extremely high while the winter weather was harsh, and the feeling of isolation would often enter my body through the freezing air that came from Lake Michigan. I doubted my decision during several nights. The peaceful atmosphere of home and my father's evening prayers, which brought serenity to our house every night, were what I missed most along with my family. The absence of these familiar sounds made my nights seem completely hollow. The silence taught me to develop my personal prayer practice. I began to say my own bedtime prayers while crying as I asked God to show me the way and give me strength. The quiet moments helped me rebuild my faith through personal discovery of divine support instead of relying on external guidance.

I enrolled in a community college with hopes of studying nursing. The ability to help others has always been a natural talent for me and healthcare provides a way to create meaningful changes. The actual conditions turned out to be more difficult than I had predicted. The combination of my school work and part-time employment and financial obligations made me feel exhausted while I questioned my ability to handle everything. I failed a few exams, not because I didn't try, but because I was overwhelmed. I stayed determined to continue my fight. The memory of my father's belief and my mother's ability to endure stayed with me during every difficult moment. God gave me a purpose so quitting was not an option according to their teachings.

Eventually, I found work in a small healthcare support role at a local facility. The position lacked excitement but it provided me with an honest way to earn money and made me feel part of a community. Through nursing, I developed the ability to comfort patients by listening and showing compassion, even when my heart felt exhausted. The initial positions I held helped me develop both my professional skills and spiritual growth. I discovered that God sent me to this place to accomplish more than financial gain because I needed to learn how to serve others. The patients I encountered taught me that healing needs more than medical treatment because it requires both presence and prayer and love.

Living in Chicago also taught me independence. Through my life in Chicago, I developed self-reliance abilities. I developed personal care skills and financial management abilities and learned to deal with everyday life responsibilities. The training gave me more than just useful skills because it deepened my faith in God to an extent, I never thought possible. The path forward became visible to me because of my faith during times when I felt completely lost. I noticed God's presence in everyday occurrences such as when strangers offered me kindness and when unexpected opportunities showed up and when I found tranquility following challenging workdays. The events exceeded random coincidences because they proved that I still had someone by my side.

As time went on, the girl who had once doubted her place in the world began to see herself as a woman with purpose. Chicago wasn't just a new city; it was a spiritual classroom. Through its challenges, I found discipline. Through its loneliness, I found prayer. Through its opportunities, I found courage. God was reshaping me quietly, preparing me for something greater than I could yet understand.

Looking back now, I realize that my move to Chicago wasn't just a change in location; it was a divine appointment. The place served as the location where my religious beliefs developed as I learned to have faith during uncertain times and discovered my true calling in life. The experience taught me to surrender rather than fight for survival which I initially expected. The fresh start I encountered back then turned out to be the initial movement God made to establish my life as proof of His mercy.

CHAPTER 3

FINDING PURPOSE IN HEALTHCARE

Advocate Christ Medical Center had an unexpected impact on both my professional and spiritual growth from the moment I began working there. At that time, I saw it as a job, a way to provide for myself and my children, yet God had a much greater plan hidden in those hospital walls. The hospital environment welcomed me with its first sight of my ID badge, along with the sound of machines, the smell of antiseptic, and the steady footsteps that filled the corridors. The experience showed me a world where people fought against death while seeking salvation through faith, and it became clear that God would use this place to continue developing my life mission.

Working in healthcare is not for the faint of heart. The daily routine brought fresh obstacles, which taught me new knowledge about human life vulnerability. I witnessed joy and sorrow, healing and loss, and through it all, I learned the value of presence, simply being there when someone needed comfort. The intense suffering of my patients became unbearable at times, so I retreated to solitary spaces where I prayed for inner strength. I learned that even in a place filled with science and medicine, faith still had a place. God was there, moving through every patient's story, every recovery, and even every goodbye.

The work operated at a high speed while maintaining challenging work requirements. My physical and mental endurance faced extreme testing because of the extended work hours. The days when I felt completely drained made the constant monitor alarms sound like an inescapable melody. But no matter how weary I became, there was always something or someone that reminded me why I was there. The moments when I experienced peace through God's work, and the support of my colleagues, and the smiles of patients made the most meaningful impact on me. My job transformed into a spiritual calling which enabled me to serve people through my work. And serve God at the same time.

At the start of my hospital career, I doubted my strength to handle the ongoing requirements of this healthcare environment. The stress and emotional impact, along with the distressing patient stories, made me feel exhausted at times. God used every challenge I faced to improve my character. I discovered fresh ways to rely on Him through my requests for steady hands during emergencies, and enduring patience when I faced exhaustion. Through his testing of me, He developed my ability to endure. I learned that perseverance requires more than determination, because it needs faith in God's ability to lead us through difficult times.

Over time, I grew into my role. My coworkers became like family a mix of personalities and hearts who shared one goal: to help others heal. We laughed together during quiet nights and supported each other through moments of loss. I realized that healthcare was more than a system; it was a community built on compassion. And within that community, I found my calling not just to care for patients but to bring light into their darkest hours.

I experienced numerous instances where God revealed Himself through tiny and seemingly unnoticeable signs. A patient who had been unresponsive suddenly opened their eyes and smiled. A family who had lost hope began to pray again. The process of healing taught me that it appears in different ways because physical healing occurs alongside emotional, and spiritual healing. God's hand was always at work, even in moments that looked like defeat.

My time at Advocate Christ Medical Center taught me both discipline and humility. The experience demonstrated to me how determination leads to success while showing the value of caring for others. The most important service we offer people comes from simple caring actions, which prove their existence matters to others. My soul developed through the combination of long nights, tears, and exhaustion, which formed its training ground. The tests of each day forced me to grow. Yet they also strengthened my dedication to my mission.

Working in healthcare also helped me grow personally. I developed patience and understanding through my experiences while learning about human life vulnerability. The experience of watching people in their most defenseless moments made me see the value of every single day. It reminded me that we are all dependent on grace no matter our status, strength, or title. The experience taught me to find God outside church walls because I experienced His presence in hospital rooms and waiting areas, and in every miraculous heartbeat.

Looking back, I now see that those years were a divine classroom. The lessons weren't always easy, but they were essential. The hospital became a sacred place where I not only worked, but also worshipped through service. The process of becoming my true self happened through God's work in me, which showed itself in every kind deed and every prayer spoken in church. Every tear fell at a patient's bedside.

My work in healthcare went beyond employment because it served as my life mission. The place became my training ground to develop discipline and compassion, while learning to maintain faith during difficult times. God used the hospital to develop my professional abilities, yet He revealed my life mission through this experience. Through service, I found strength. Through struggle, I found grace. Through every challenge, I found Him.

CHAPTER 4

MOTHERHOOD, SACRIFICE, AND STRENGTH

Becoming a mother changed everything about who I was and how I saw the world. When I first held my daughter, Alexis, I felt a love so deep it seemed to touch every part of my soul. Later, when my son, Tyree, was born, that love expanded beyond anything I thought possible. Motherhood was both the greatest joy and the greatest responsibility I would ever know. It brought light into my life but also tested every part of my strength, patience, and faith.

Raising two children on my own was never easy. The road was filled with long nights, endless worries, and sacrifices that only a mother's heart could understand. I worked tirelessly to provide stability for Alexis and Tyree not just a roof over our heads, but a sense of safety and love they could depend on. There were times when money was tight, when bills piled up faster than I could pay them, and when exhaustion seemed to be my only constant companion. Yet through it all, I kept reminding myself that God had trusted me with these two precious lives. That thought alone gave me the courage to keep moving forward even when I felt I had nothing left to give.

Many nights, I would stay awake after they had fallen asleep, watching them breathe softly, thanking God for their presence in my life. Those quiet hours often became my prayer time. I asked for strength to guide them, for wisdom to make the right choices, and for protection over their futures. There were nights when tears fell silently because I felt the weight of responsibility pressing down on me, but even then, God's peace would find me. Somehow, He always provided maybe not in the way I expected, but always right on time.

Motherhood taught me more about faith than any sermon ever could. It showed me that love requires endurance and that real strength often comes in moments of weakness. There were days I felt completely drained, running between work, home, and the endless needs of my children. I would look at my paycheck and wonder how it would stretch far enough, or how I would keep up with everything. But each challenge reminded me that God was still in control. Every time I reached my breaking point, He sent a small miracle an unexpected opportunity, a kind word, or a moment of peace that gave me just enough energy to go on.

As Alexis and Tyree grew, I learned that motherhood isn't only about providing; it's about shaping hearts. I wanted them to see the importance of kindness, integrity, and faith, even when life was hard. I didn't have all the answers, but I had love and I gave it to them in every way I could. Whether it was helping with homework after a long shift or sitting beside them during their toughest moments, I tried to show them that love and prayer can carry you through anything.

There were times I questioned myself, wondering if I was doing enough or being enough. Single motherhood often brings loneliness that others don't see a silence that follows after the house grows still. But in those moments, I turned to God for reassurance. He reminded me that even when I felt alone, I was never truly by myself. His strength filled the spaces where mine ran out.

Over the years, I began to see how each sacrifice was not in vain. My children became my motivation, my daily reminder of God's faithfulness. Their laughter filled the house, turning our small home into a sanctuary of love. They didn't need perfection; they needed presence and that, I could give them. Watching them grow taught me the value of every sleepless night, every prayer whispered through tears, and every decision made in faith.

Motherhood was my greatest teacher. It humbled me, stretched me, and brought me closer to God than ever before. It taught me patience I didn't know I had and strength I didn't believe was possible. I learned to find beauty in the struggle and to thank God not just for the victories, but for the hard days that built my character.

Looking back, I realize that every sacrifice I made was a seed planted in love. God used those years to refine me, to mold me into a woman who could endure and still give with an open heart. The sleepless nights became lessons in trust. The tears became prayers. And the struggles became testimonies of grace.

Through motherhood, I discovered a deeper understanding of God's love the kind that never gives up, never runs out, and never stops believing. My journey as a mother has been marked by challenges, but it has also been blessed by faith, joy, and unshakable love. And though the road was far from easy, I wouldn't trade a single moment, because it was through motherhood that I found the truest reflection of strength the kind that comes only from God.

CHAPTER 5

A SON'S CHALLENGE, A MOTHER'S FAITH

When my son, Tyree, was born, I felt the same joy and wonder that fills every mother's heart when she first hears her child's cry. But soon after, that joy was tested in ways I never imagined. The doctors' faces were calm but serious, their words heavy and hard to accept. They told me my son had cerebral palsy. In that moment, time seemed to stop. The room around me faded, and all I could hear was the pounding of my own heart. I remember holding Tyree close, staring at his tiny face, and whispering a prayer. I didn't know what the future would hold, but I knew I couldn't let fear take control.

Those early days were filled with uncertainty. I went from dreaming about my son's first steps to fearing he might never take them. There were nights I cried quietly, not out of weakness, but out of love a love so deep it broke my heart and healed it at the same time. I prayed for strength, for wisdom, and for peace, because I knew I couldn't walk this road alone. God became my anchor when the waves of worry tried to drown me.

The months that followed were filled with doctor appointments, therapy sessions, and long hours in hospital waiting rooms. Each visit brought a new list of challenges and medical terms I had to learn. There were moments when hope seemed far away, but I refused to give in to despair. I made a choice early on to focus on what Tyree could do, not what he couldn't. I began to see God's hand in every small victory every smile, every sound, every moment of calm. Those moments reminded me that progress is measured not only in milestones, but in faith.

Caring for Tyree required a strength I didn't know I had. There were nights when exhaustion pressed on me so hard that I would fall asleep in a hospital chair, holding his hand. There were times I questioned whether I was doing enough, whether I was strong enough. But every time I reached that breaking point, I felt God whisper to my heart, "You're not alone. I am with you." His voice gave me the courage to face each new day.

I learned that faith isn't just believing that God can change your circumstances it's trusting Him even when He doesn't. There were prayers that went unanswered, at least in the way I hoped. But over time, I realized that God was answering in other ways giving me patience when I was tired, peace when I was anxious, and perseverance when I felt like giving up. My son's life became a daily reminder that God's grace is not measured by what we receive, but by how we endure with love.

Tyree taught me more about faith than any sermon ever could. His spirit, even in pain, carried a quiet strength. There were days when his smile was brighter than my own, reminding me that joy doesn't come from perfection, it comes from presence. Watching him fight through every therapy, every challenge, I saw what true courage looked like. And as his mother, I learned that love is not about fixing everything, it's about standing beside someone through everything.

Being Tyree's mother deepened my faith in ways words can hardly express. I began to see miracles not as grand gestures, but as small mercies scattered through our days. The nurse who offered comfort when I was overwhelmed, the doctor who prayed quietly before a procedure, the unexpected strength that came when I felt like collapsing those were miracles. God was there, working through the hands and hearts of people around us, reminding me that He never leaves His children.

There were moments when I felt invisible to the world tired, drained, and unseen. But even in those moments, I learned that God sees the quiet warriors, the mothers who keep pushing forward when no one is watching. He sees the tears we wipe away before our children notice. He sees the prayers we whisper in the dark. And He turns those tears into strength, those prayers into power.

Looking back now, I realize that Tyree's diagnosis didn't define our lives it refined them. It taught me compassion, humility, and endurance. It taught me to find beauty in the struggle and strength in surrender. Through my son's journey, I learned that life doesn't have to be perfect to be purposeful. Every challenge, every sleepless night, every prayer uttered through tears became part of a bigger plan a plan designed not to break me, but to build me.

Tyree's life has been both my greatest challenge and my greatest blessing. Through him, I witnessed what it means to live with grace under pressure. His courage inspired my faith to grow stronger, deeper, and more real. I no longer see our story as one of struggle, but as a testimony of God's faithfulness.

Through my son's challenge, I discovered a mother's faith not fragile or fleeting, but fierce and unwavering. The road was hard, but it led me closer to God. And though I once feared what our future would hold, I now see it as a journey of love, perseverance, and divine purpose. Through Tyree, God taught me that even in the hardest seasons, His grace is always enough.

CHAPTER 6

HEARTBREAK, BETRAYAL, AND RESILIENCE

I never imagined that love something meant to bring warmth and comfort could also bring so much pain. When I entered that relationship, my heart was open, hopeful, and ready to believe in love again. I thought I had found someone who understood me, someone who would appreciate the woman I had become after years of struggle and sacrifice. At first, everything seemed perfect. The words were kind, the gestures thoughtful, and the promises convincing. I believed them all, because I wanted to believe that God had finally sent me a partner who would stand beside me.

But over time, the truth began to reveal itself. The man who once spoke with tenderness now used words like weapons. The affection that once felt genuine turned cold and manipulative. I started to see the signs of control the way he twisted my words, the way he made me doubt my own worth, the way he turned every situation into my fault. I realized I wasn't loved; I was being used. It was as if I had stepped into a storm I never saw coming, one that tore at my confidence and left me questioning everything I knew about love.

There were days when I couldn't recognize myself. I tried so hard to keep the peace, to make things right, to prove that I was enough. But the harder I tried, the more I lost pieces of myself. The relationship became a cycle of hope and heartbreak apologies followed by more pain, promises followed by disappointment. I found myself praying through tears, asking God why love had turned into suffering. And though I couldn't see it at the time, He was already working on my escape, guiding me out of the darkness one painful step at a time.

The betrayal cut deep. Trust, once broken, doesn't heal overnight. There were moments when I felt completely rejected not just by a man, but by life itself. The loneliness that followed was heavy. I remember coming home after long shifts, walking into an empty room, and feeling the silence echo around me. Yet even in that emptiness, God met me. He didn't shout over the silence; He whispered into it. His voice reminded me that I was still His child, still loved, still worthy. Slowly, I began to understand that the relationship hadn't broken me it had revealed what was already whole within me.

Healing didn't happen all at once. It came through long nights of reflection, through journaling, prayer, and tears. I had to face the truth not only about the man who hurt me but also about the parts of myself that had settled for less than I deserved. I learned that loving someone else should never mean losing yourself in the process. Real love builds, it doesn't break. Real love reflects God's heart, not manipulation or control. That realization changed everything.

In the midst of heartbreak, God began restoring what had been taken from me my identity, my peace, my confidence. I learned to see myself again through His eyes, not through the lens of someone else's cruelty. I stopped asking, "Why did this happen to me?" and started asking, "What is God trying to teach me through this?" That shift in perspective gave me freedom. I began to walk with my head a little higher, my spirit a little lighter.

I found strength in places I didn't know existed. My pain became my teacher. It showed me how resilient the human heart can be when faith is its foundation. Each day I reminded myself that God had delivered me before, and He would do it again. Slowly, the anger faded, and forgiveness began to take its place not because he deserved it, but because I refused to let bitterness hold me captive.

Through heartbreak, I discovered the beauty of starting over. I realized that endings are not always failures; sometimes they are divine redirections. God used that relationship to open my eyes to patterns of brokenness that needed to be healed. He showed me that I didn't need to be validated by anyone else's approval, I was already complete in Him.

Looking back now, I can see that what felt like destruction was actually deliverance. The relationship that once drained me became the turning point that restored me. It taught me that love without respect isn't love at all, and that heartbreak can become holy ground when you let God stand with you in it.

Through betrayal, I found clarity. Through pain, I found purpose. And through heartbreak, I found resilience, not the kind that hardens your heart, but the kind that softens it with wisdom and faith. I emerged from that season stronger, wiser, and closer to God than ever before. He turned what was meant to break me into a lesson that rebuilt me. And for that, I no longer see the story as one of loss, but one of grace because even in heartbreak, God's love never left me.

CHAPTER 7

RISING AGAIN THROUGH FAITH AND WORK

After walking through the storms of heartbreak and loss, I reached a point where I knew something inside me had to change. I couldn't stay in that place of pain forever. I had cried enough tears to fill a river, but even rivers move forward they don't stay still. It was time to rise again, to rebuild, and to believe that God still had a plan for my life. I didn't know how everything would come together, but I trusted that if I kept moving in faith, God would meet me on the journey.

The first step was rebuilding my confidence not just as a woman, but as a child of God. My heart was still tender, but my spirit had grown stronger through everything I had endured. I prayed daily for direction, asking God to show me where to start. Slowly, doors began to open. A new job opportunity appeared, one that allowed me to step into a position with greater responsibility and better pay. It wasn't just a promotion in my career it was a sign of divine restoration.

Work became both my focus and my healing ground. The same way God had used the hospital years earlier to shape my purpose, He now used my career to rebuild my life. I threw myself into my duties with renewed energy, determined to prove that my past would not define my future. There were long days and endless tasks, but every effort felt meaningful because I was building something new stability, self-worth, and a sense of peace that came from trusting God's timing.

Financial stability didn't happen overnight, but it came faster than I expected. I went from struggling to make ends meet to watching God multiply what little I had. Each paycheck reminded me of His faithfulness. I began paying off debts, saving for the future, and finally feeling the weight of survival begin to lift. I knew this wasn't luck or coincidence it was God rewarding the faith that had carried me through the valley.

But success wasn't just about the money. It was about the strength I discovered in the process. For the first time in years, I felt proud of myself not for achieving perfection, but for enduring the process of becoming whole. I learned to celebrate progress instead of waiting for everything to be perfect. My work became an expression of gratitude every task, every hour, every new challenge was a way to say, *"Thank You, Lord, for another chance."*

Even in my professional success, I never forgot where I came from or what I had survived. I carried the lessons of loss, betrayal, and motherhood with me into every space I entered. They kept me humble and grounded. When others complained about their workload, I silently thanked God that I even had a job to go to. When new challenges came, I reminded myself that I had faced harder things and come out stronger. My faith had taught me that no position, no paycheck, no title could ever compare to peace.

As my career grew, so did my purpose. I found myself mentoring others, encouraging coworkers, and offering words of comfort to those going through difficult times. It became clear that my journey wasn't just about me it was about using my story to lift others up. God had restored me so I could help others see that restoration was possible for them too.

There were still moments of loneliness, of quiet reflection, when I would think about everything I had lost relationships, time, and dreams that didn't unfold as planned. But instead of feeling bitter, I felt grateful. I realized that every broken piece had been used to build a stronger version of me. What once felt like punishment was really preparation. Every setback had been setting me up for this moment a season of stability, strength, and peace.

I began to see my work as more than a job it became a testimony. Each time I walked through those doors, I remembered the woman who once cried herself to sleep, unsure if she would ever recover. Now I stood with confidence, not because of my own power, but because of God's grace. He had carried me from surviving to thriving, and every success was a reflection of His hand on my life.

Looking back now, I see that this chapter of my life was never just about career advancement it was about spiritual restoration. God rebuilt me from the inside out. Through work, He gave me purpose. Through faith, He gave me peace. Through perseverance, He gave me provision. What the enemy meant to destroy, God used to elevate.

I learned that rising again doesn't always mean returning to what you lost sometimes it means becoming something entirely new. My story became living proof that no matter how far you fall, with faith, you can always rise again. The same God who saw me in heartbreak also saw me in healing, and through His grace, I rose stronger, wiser, and ready for whatever came next.

CHAPTER 8

THE AWAKENING OF THE CHOSEN ONE

There comes a moment in every believer's life when faith moves from being something you practice to something you live. For me, that moment came when I realized that everything I had endured the pain, the losses, the victories had not been random. They were all pieces of a divine plan meant to awaken me to who I truly was. I was not just a survivor of life's storms; I was one of God's chosen.

It began quietly, not with a miracle or a vision, but with a stirring deep within my spirit. After all the battles I had faced heartbreak, loneliness, and rebuilding I started to sense that God was calling me into something greater. I began spending more time in prayer, seeking understanding, asking God to show me what He wanted from my life. Each prayer felt like a conversation, not just a request. I could feel His presence more deeply than ever before, guiding me gently toward purpose.

One Sunday morning, I decided to be baptized again not because I doubted my salvation, but because I wanted to renew my commitment. I wanted to wash away the remnants of pain and walk fully in the identity God had given me. As I stepped into the water, I felt an overwhelming peace settle over me. It was as if every wound, every burden, every unanswered question was lifted away. When I came up from the water, I knew something inside me had changed. I wasn't the same woman who had entered that pool I had been reborn with clarity and conviction.

That moment marked the beginning of my spiritual awakening. I started to see my life differently. The hardships I once resented became the very experiences that equipped me for my calling. I realized that God had allowed certain storms not to destroy me but to strengthen me. My testimony wasn't meant to stay hidden; it was meant to shine so that others could see what faith could do.

With that revelation came responsibility. Carrying God's light in a dark world isn't easy. I soon learned that not everyone would understand my transformation. Some people from my past looked at me with skepticism, questioning my faith and my purpose. Others drifted away when my focus shifted from worldly goals to spiritual growth. At first, that rejection hurt but then I understood that not everyone can walk with you once God begins to elevate you. Sometimes separation is protection.

There were days when the enemy tried to make me doubt myself, whispering lies that I wasn't worthy or capable. But through prayer and Scripture, I found strength to silence those voices. I clung to verses that reminded me of who I was in Christ chosen, redeemed, and set apart. Whenever fear crept in, I reminded myself that God doesn't call the qualified; He qualifies the called. That truth gave me courage to keep walking in obedience, even when the path felt lonely.

The more I sought God, the clearer my purpose became. I began sharing my testimony more openly not for attention, but to give hope. I wanted others to know that God's grace can rebuild any life, no matter how broken it once was. I started volunteering, mentoring, and encouraging women who had faced similar struggles. Each time I spoke, I could feel the Holy Spirit move through me, reminding me that this was the reason for everything I had gone through. I was not just meant to survive I was meant to serve.

My awakening also came with a new sense of discernment. I became more aware of the spiritual battles around me the negativity, the temptations, the distractions that tried to pull me away from my purpose. It wasn't always easy to walk in light when the world around me seemed consumed by darkness. But I learned that shining light doesn't mean you have to be perfect; it means you keep reflecting God's love even when it's hard. My faith became my armor, and prayer became my constant companion.

There were moments of deep solitude during this time times when I felt isolated, misunderstood, or even spiritually weary. But those moments taught me that being chosen isn't always about being celebrated; sometimes it's about being set apart. God was teaching me to depend on Him completely, to trust His voice above all others. I realized that the calling He placed on my life was not for comfort, but for purpose.

Looking back, I can see how everything in my journey led me to this awakening. The struggles that once brought me to my knees were the very moments that brought me closer to God. The heartbreak that tried to break me instead built my faith. The seasons of silence prepared me to hear His voice more clearly. I finally understood that I wasn't just living I was walking in divine purpose.

Through baptism, prayer, and revelation, God showed me who I was meant to be. He didn't just heal me; He transformed me. I no longer saw myself as the woman who had been through pain, but as the woman chosen to turn that pain into purpose. My life was no longer about survival it was about service.

The awakening of the chosen one wasn't a single moment; it was the unfolding of everything God had been preparing me for all along. And now, when I look in the mirror, I see not what I've lost, but what God has restored. My heart carries peace, my hands carry purpose, and my voice carries the story of a woman who learned that being chosen by God is not about perfection it's about surrender.

CHAPTER 9

WALKING IN PURPOSE AND SERVICE

When God reveals your purpose, life begins to take on a new meaning. The same world that once felt heavy with pain now feels filled with opportunity not for personal gain, but for giving. After my spiritual awakening, I understood that every struggle I had endured wasn't just about me. It was about preparing me to serve others. God had taken my story of survival and turned it into a message of hope. I was no longer walking in brokenness; I was walking in purpose.

My days began to look different. I started each morning with prayer, not just asking for blessings but asking how I could be a blessing. That shift changed everything. I began volunteering in my community, helping wherever there was need from serving food at local shelters to speaking at women's groups about faith and resilience. Every time I shared my testimony, I saw pieces of myself reflected in the faces of those listening. Their tears, their nods, their smiles reminded me that pain can become a bridge connecting hearts that understand one another through God's grace.

Mentoring young women became one of my greatest joys. Many of them came from hard places broken homes, financial struggles, self-doubt the same battles I once faced. I wanted them to see that faith could lift them higher than any circumstance. I told them that the same God who carried me through storms could carry them too. When I saw their eyes light up with new hope, I knew I was exactly where I was meant to be. It wasn't about titles or recognition; it was about obedience.

Service gave me peace in a way nothing else ever had. Helping others reminded me of how far God had brought me and how faithful He continued to be. Each act of service no matter how small became a form of worship. Whether it was praying for a stranger, mentoring a single mother, or simply offering words of encouragement, I felt God's presence in it all. The more I gave, the more joy I received. It was as if every time I poured out love, God filled me right back up.

Of course, walking in purpose wasn't without challenges. There were times I grew tired or felt overlooked. Sometimes the very people I tried to help rejected my kindness or questioned my motives. But I learned that service isn't about being thanked it's about being faithful. God reminded me that obedience matters more than applause. So even when no one noticed, I kept serving. I kept showing up, trusting that every small act of kindness was seen by the One who called me to do it.

As I continued to serve, I began to understand something deeper: my testimony wasn't just a story it was a ministry. Every pain, every prayer, every miracle became part of the message God wanted me to share. He had transformed my life so that others could see what transformation looked like through Him. My mission became simple to inspire and uplift through faith, honesty, and love.

Giving back to my community also gave me a sense of belonging I hadn't felt in years. It was no longer about chasing success or recognition; it was about planting seeds of hope. Sometimes that meant giving my time, sometimes my resources, and often my heart. There is a special kind of peace that comes from knowing you're living in alignment with your purpose. I didn't have to search for meaning anymore I was living it every day.

Through this new season, I saw how God works in cycles of restoration. The same girl who once felt broken now helped others heal. The same woman who once cried alone in prayer now prayed for others to find strength. That's the beauty of God's grace He doesn't just lift you up; He positions you to lift others. I finally understood that service isn't a duty; it's a privilege.

Looking back, I can see how far God has brought me from pain to peace, from surviving to serving, from searching to fulfilling. Walking in purpose means living each day with intention, knowing that even the smallest act of love can echo through eternity. My story is no longer one of struggle, but of surrender the kind that leads to transformation and freedom.

Today, I live with gratitude, carrying the lessons of my journey as reminders of God's faithfulness. Every time I help someone, speak encouragement, or pray for another, I feel His light guiding me. I don't walk alone anymore I walk in step with Him. My purpose is not just to tell my story, but to use it to remind others that no matter where they've been, God can still use them.

Through faith, I found my strength. Through service, I found my peace. And through obedience, I found my calling. My life is no longer about what I've endured, but about what God continues to do through me. This is what it means to walk in purpose to live each day as a vessel of His light, serving others with a heart that knows where it's been and Who brought it through.

CHAPTER 10

HOME AT LAST; ACCEPTING THE LOVE OF CHRIST

Accepting the love of Christ is one of the most beautiful and life-changing experiences a person can have. For so many years, I walked through life thinking I was completely alone that I had to fight every battle by myself. My mind was restless, my heart uncertain, and my emotions scattered in every direction. I was surviving, not living. Each day felt like a climb up a mountain that never ended. Depression, anxiety, and exhaustion shadowed my steps. I was doing everything I could to hold life together for myself and my two children, but inside, I was falling apart.

I remember those long nights when I would stare at the ceiling and wonder what I was doing wrong. I worked hard, I paid the bills, I made sure my children ate, but something in me was missing. My heart felt hollow. I didn't understand that what I was truly searching for wasn't stability it was peace. And that peace could only come from one place: the love of Christ. Looking back, I can see now that even in my confusion, even in my darkest hours, Jesus was there. He was protecting me, providing for me, and patiently waiting for me to stop running and turn toward Him.

At the time, I didn't realize I was drowning. I thought I was managing life just fine keeping busy, pushing through, smiling when I needed to. But deep down, I was struggling to stay afloat. The truth is, sometimes you can be so lost in the motions of survival that you don't even notice you're sinking. Life felt like a roller coaster one moment up, the next down and I couldn't find my balance. But Christ was there, steady and unchanging, offering me a peace the world couldn't give.

I had to learn the hard way that we were never meant to live life alone. Jesus doesn't promise us a life free from struggle, but He does promise us the strength to face it and the kind of love that never fails. His love is not like human love; it doesn't depend on performance or perfection. It is everlasting, unconditional, and pure. That realization became my turning point. I finally understood that I didn't have to fight for love I only had to accept it.

When I began my spiritual growth journey, it started small quiet moments of prayer, a few minutes of reading Scripture, and trying to sit still in silence. It wasn't easy. I had relied on distractions for so long people, television, social media anything that kept me from being alone with my thoughts. But the more I chose silence, the more I felt His presence. I realized that the noise I had been avoiding wasn't just around me; it was within me. And in that stillness, God began to heal me from the inside out.

I started setting daily spiritual patterns prayer in the morning, meditation in the afternoon, gratitude in the evening. Sometimes, I did it minute by minute just to stay grounded. I didn't invite anyone into that process because I needed time to hear from God without interference. It was lonely at first, but necessary. I had to learn how to be comfortable with my own company and how to listen to His voice without distractions.

Then one day, something changed. It wasn't dramatic or loud it was gentle, but unmistakable. While watching a sermon online, the speaker began talking about the very thing I had prayed about the night before. Word for word, it felt as if God Himself was answering me.

Tears filled my eyes. In that moment, I knew He was real, He was listening, and He had been with me all along.

From that day forward, everything in my life began to shift. I trusted Him more. I prayed with greater faith. I stopped relying on my own understanding and started depending on His guidance. Slowly, I began to see transformation not just in my circumstances, but in my spirit. I found peace where there used to be panic. I found balance where there used to be confusion. I found purpose where there used to be pain. Jesus wasn't a distant figure anymore; He was my companion, my counselor, my peace.

I learned that Christ doesn't judge us for where we've been He celebrates who we can become through Him. He knows every fear, every failure, every hidden wound, and still calls us His own. Through His grace, I found wholeness in my mind, spirit, and soul. I discovered that true healing isn't about escaping pain but inviting Him into it. When I finally surrendered, He filled every empty space in me with love, purpose, and light.

Today, I live differently. My days are still busy, but they're no longer empty. I've learned to keep my spiritual growth first prayer before plans, faith before fear, peace before pressure. I stay in His presence because that's where I find strength. I'm home now not in a physical sense, but in my spirit. I've found the place where my soul rests in Christ Jesus.

If you're reading this and you're tired, broken, or lost if you've been wondering whether life can get better I promise you it can. Call on Jesus. Talk to Him, even if you don't know what to say. He's been listening all along. He will meet you right where you are, no matter what you've done or how far you've drifted. His love doesn't expire, and His arms are always open.

I look at my life now my peace, my strength, my purpose and I can't help but give thanks. Jesus didn't just save me from the storm; He taught me how to walk on the water with Him. He turned my fear into faith, my sorrow into joy, and my confusion into clarity. I am living proof that His love changes everything.

Christ Jesus is real. He lives. He restores. And He still saves. I'm home at last safe in His love, anchored in His grace, and walking in the truth that I was never alone.

CONCLUSION

LIVING AS A LIGHT IN DARK TIMES

Spiritual growth can improve our Emotional and Physical WELL-BEING. Spiritual GROWTH helps me to develop healthy habits that lowers my stress level. I incorporate these Practices—through Prayer, Deep Breathing and Meditation Exercises. I'm not so easily reactive to negativity, as I go out in the World to interact anywhere I go. I try now to keep my surroundings in a Positive Environment. Increasing our Spiritual Growth allows us to be able to handle any given situation at hand; we can change us, even if the World doesn't.

Incorporating these practices brings a sense of self-awareness, it helps me to pay attention to my negative mindset. For me, in order for me to build & maintain these practices, I incorporate a positive mindset. I'm able to identify with my true authentic self. I'm honest when I approach those things that may be interfering or taking me away from God. If there's any part of me I'm not honest with myself and know inside, I have become who God created me to be. If I'm too focused on myself or worried over who I am, I can always go to God, and He opens my heart and mind to what's real and what's not.

I must know Who I am and Whose I am, which is a Child of God, we are all Children of the Almighty High. To me knowing who I am has helped me to stay grounded and disciplined; it has helped that I had to identify with what had to stay and what had to go with my deepest energy.

Deepening My Connections

I had to build a true relationship with god, I always was staggering on the ungodly side of things, only going to church on Sundays or reading the Bible only on Sundays or when things got bad for me. That's when I knew I needed God the most, and not realizing that God was always with me through the good and the bad. I started paying attention to my surroundings, what I was doing day by day. I really had to give up the TV life and all that surrounded me that was not bringing me any peace and joy.

It took me a while to realize that I was being disobedient, and my growth had failed. I had to strengthen my FAITH, and to build a true foundation with God. Through this I found my purpose, and I am no longer struggling in areas that had me confused. The Lord had been waiting for me to surrender fully, and when I did, He began to guide my steps. I'm learning every day to trust Him more, to walk in faith, and to remain still when I need to.

This is My Conclusion of what SPIRITUAL GROWTH looks and feels like, how you find the best in your Journey for Spiritual Growth for PEACE, LOVE and HAPPINESS. GOD Bless You!!